One in Hundred

Sreeja Gadhiraju

Presentation by *BookLeaf Publishing*

Web: www.bookleafpub.com

E-mail: info@bookleafpub.com

ISBN: 9789357445511

First edition 2021

DEDICATION

Dear Mom,

I am here only because of you.

And not only this book, but everything which is I do in life is just dedicated to you.

ACKNOWLEDGEMENT

Dear Dad,
You made me the strongest.
Though you are not with me,
I am always carrying Us with me.

PREFACE

Welcome to my world of random thoughts

One in Hundred

Yes, I am a one in hundred,
No, I am not lying I am speaking the truth,
I don't mind if the 99 of you don't understand
me,
But at least give it a try!
How can I explain it to you that the way your
brain reacts to things is different than mine?
Something which doesn't bother you at all might
create chaos within me,
And something which you don't care about at all
might make me the happiest.
Stop invalidating my feelings just because you
don't understand them,
Start being a human and learn them.
I am a borderliner,
Please don't push me across my borders.

Battle within

Here I am again,
dwelling in the darkness I have created on my
own,
hearing the chaos within my head in silence,
resilient to the shallowness crawling over,
staring at the reflecting emptiness,
fighting against loser inside,
consoling another poor soul who resides with in,
A little I know, few gulps of alcohol down the
throat shall be an escape indeed,
Yet, I aint falling for it, not again,
Alas, I don't want to escape anymore,
Rather I would fall into the pain with in,
I know the demons within wouldn't give up even
in the dreams,
Well,
May be its time for them to meet the real me.

Acknowledging the other me

It is not easy acknowledge that you have
different people residing with in,
It is not easy to accept the fact that you are not
completely you,
It is not easy to let someone know about it and
being called as crazy,
But every survivor out there are doing,
Day in and day out,
Did you ever give it a thought about why would
some one chose not to be themselves?
The answer is quite simple,
They cannot choose it.
It's not their choice.
Imagine, if you have an option to be happy and
forget everything,
Would you not make that choice?
Then what makes you think that I don't

For how long?

A ruthless brain,
An emotionless heart,
A confused soul,
A never caring pretending attitude,
A behavior which will always make you
question if you are really loved,
Not clingy,
Not cheesy,
A dangerous level of craving for adrenaline
rush,
A pain in life,
A burden on brain,
The one who might make you feel like they are
regret for a lifetime,
The combination of all possible disasters,
Will you still dare to love that human?
If you do,
For how long?

Anxiety or Depression?

Anxiety? Depression?
I don't exactly know what occurs when!
All I know is that wierd feeling in stomach,
Voices in head, Unbearable and unexplainable
feeling!
Sometimes I want to scream till my vocal cords
break, and sometimes I just want to sit in the
dark!
Sometimes I want to eat forever and sometimes
even the smell of the food makes me sick!
Those unclear voices in my head gives me so
many orders,
Sometimes I fight and sometimes I give up and
surrender so that I can make peace with them!
I end up being awake for days and sometimes I
sleep for ages,
Sometimes I fall asleep after crying and
sometimes I wake up with tears in my eyes!
And I am in a war with what's inside my head,
every single day!
Yet I don't give up!
After all, If it is strong, I am the strongest!!

Simple, Isnt it?

Smile,
Sounds simple isn't it???
Try it when you have eyes filled with tears, but
you just can't let them out!
Try it when your heart feels the heaviest even
when you are sitting idle!
Try it when you are sitting between many but
still lost in thoughts!
Try it when you are frustrated to do something
but still you have to do as you don't have an
option!
Try it when your laughter sounds stupidest and
fake to your own self!
And finally,
Try it when your optimistic dreams turn out to
realistic fate!
Now answer it again,
Smile,

Simple, isn't it???

Why?

I never understood why!
Why do I turn silence into chaos?
Why do I choose to change breeze into a
hurricane?
Why do I end up in the valley just beside a plain
road?
Why do I have to convince myself that
something is wrong when nothing is wrong?
Why do I prefer Dark whilst the light?
Why is that I had to wake up though I love the
dream?
Why do I rust where I have an option of not
losing my charm?
Why is that I think about WHY more than a
HOW?
I wish I could understand WHY!!

What if?

What if you are the darkest side of yours which
you hate,
what if you have already reached the rock
bottom when you are still thinking you are still
drowning,
what if you lost your way while you are thinking
that you are getting lost?
what if you happen to become the person whom
you would never become?
going in circles, knowing that there is no end,
what if you are holding on to something which
was long gone,
what if that something is you yourself,
what if you know that you know that there is no
"If" anymore?
what if you could not hear yourself anymore!
and
what if you get to reach the beginning which you
know is the end?
Would it hurt? Perhaps, would it hurt more than
before?

Voices within

Darkness,
Voices inside head,
whilst the depression crawls over and asks you
to go numb,
anxiousness asks you to scream and break the
bones,
words can't explain this feeling,
neither someone can see it!

They call it the "Over thinking" and without
even knowing they forces you not to talk about
it,
But trust me,
You are not alone, and the struggle is real!
The moment you accept it, you will be the best
friend you need!

You dont have to be strong

All my life,
I was busy being strong,
I stood up against grief,
I was fighting with my traumas,
I got used to that one sentence;
'You are so strong'
I never gave a chance to my traumas to explain
their side,
I haven't accepted what has happened to me,

But finally, I am glad that I realized,
I had to have an acceptance,
I had to accept mistakes as mistakes.
It's never too late,
I am done being strong,
I am not fighting with my traumas anymore,
I ma just taking those along with me with a
heartfelt acceptance.
And I am healing!

If you are there,
Thinking about traumas,

Just remember,
You don't have to be strong,
You can fall weak at times,
You can cry,
You can speak about those,

Cause running away and escaping in the name of
being strong,
Wont heal you !

Dont you let it go!

Sometimes you may feel like this is it,
Maybe you are just tired,
Maybe you are on the borderline of it,
Maybe you are thinking that there is nothing
forward,

Then take a long pause,
Breath,
See how far you came,
How many hurdles you overcame?

Wherever you are, look around,
No matter how much of a darkness you are
surrounded with,
There shall be a ray of light, and that's you.

You are the beacon of your life love,
Don't you let it go!
I understand it may sometimes take everything
you have,
But still,
Don't you let it go!

Life goes on!

Life goes on!

Dwelling in memories,
Walking past the present souvenirs,
Life goes on!

Cursing through the heartbreaks ,
Wiping up the rolling tears,
Life goes on!

Cherishing up the big laughs,
Wondering about the happy tears,
Life goes on!

Wowing about the adventures,
Giggling about those freak shows,
Remembering the strangers' faces,
Swiping through a number of galleries,
LIFE JUST GOES ON!

Dear you!

Dear you,
I know it has been difficult,
I know you feel like the world has been turned
upside down,
I know that you feel lost,
I know that you feel different,
But dear you,
You are not alone in this!
People lost their loved ones, opportunities!
The world is struggling along with you,
While the positivity flooding over social media,
While the colorful pictures of updates fill your
screen,
Let me tell you, people would choose to pretend
than accept,
And dear you, it's okay to be on the other side!
It's okay to be lost,
It's okay to be path less,
It's okay to be the odd one out!
And

It's really okay to be not okay!
Breath in and trust the universe!
Because, when you know that it's all gone,
You also know that you won't lose anything else
And
It's gonna get just better!

A letter to me, from me!

You have been made fun of,
Your character was judged,
Your honesty was questioned,
Your intentions were suspected,
Your behavior was unexpected,
You were respected,
Meanwhile you were never understood,
You were lost,
Meanwhile you have never been found,
But you got all love of mine,
You are the best and you will always be!
Don't let anything bring you down,
After all, the only thing which I could never get
over is your fighting spirit,
Yes, I failed you a couple of times,
I might let you down sometimes,
But I always got your back!
Spread your wings darling,
I have got your back!
- To me from ME

You are not perfect!

You are not perfect,
You are an absolute mess of confused thoughts,
You make mistakes,
You walk the wrong paths,
You throw your words in the wrong direction,
You hurt people, you trust the wrong ones,
You cry, you scream, and have lost nights,
You laugh at the Woods and stare at the
darkness,
None of these makes you any less of a human!
They make you an incredible one!

Lost nights

Coldhearted, headstrong, emotionless, Lunatic!!!
There she was,
In a dark place of smoke,
The coffin made of stones she built herself,
Sealed with the cement of broken hopes!
She sits with demons of darkness coz they are no longer her foes!
She seeks anything no more!
After all, there's nothing to lose anymore!!!

Yours truly

Dear human,

I know that you hate me for what I do to you. I know that you are afraid of me too. But one can never change their own nature, can they? I meant to be this way. But I really want to help you to get rid of me.

I hear many of u saying, time heals me, but the answer is NO. It just makes you habituated to me!

Don't let me drive you! You will go nuts if you do!

You know I come with an enormous energy, but you always ignore that and concentrates on me only! Trust me, you will be the strongest if you can realize and get hold of my companion!

Finally, You always try to escape! Don't! coz
there is no way, you can just accept and
embrace!

Yours truly,
PAIN

Her thoughts!

My existence is such a big question,
It always wonders me how can I coexist with
her.
Our choices are different,
Our ideologies are different,
I hated her the most,
But now she makes a lot of sense to me,
Would I be able to survive in this heinous
world?
She understands me these days, she asks for my
opinions,
I started respecting her somehow,
I don't want to be a victim again,
I know my dreams would never be real,
But maybe it's for our own good.
For the first time, I am not angry with her,
Maybe all she is trying is to keep us alive.

Dear Society

Dear society,
What are you upto?
When you don't know what mental illness is,
When you don't know what are depression and
anxiety,
Who gives you an authority to be a critic?
Let me talk to you about some facts,
I have walked that path,
I was scared of you because of which I behaved,
Just for being different, you gave me names
even before I knew the meanings of most of
them,
I tried,
I kept on trying!
But no, you gave me no consideration,
Like every other struggler, I tried too,
I tried talking, I tried explaining what I felt,
You called it over thinking,
You asked me reasons,
You asked me why?
How can I answer that when I don't have it for
my own self?
Then I realized,
I can choose to escape!
And then I CHANGED!

Again same question, why?
I chose not to answer it anymore.
I struggled, and I am fighting as much as I
could!
If you don't understand it, it's okay,
But don't add one more reason to my bucket, it is
already full!
If some thing happens to me, don't make me a
hashtag,
Don't speak about my stories which you have no
idea about,
Respect the choices, and remember that I tried
more than you could imagine!
If you see any "Other me", please don't treat
them like you treated me!
I know the value of one life,
But before talking about mine, please make sure
you know the value of it!
Believe it or not,
The struggle is real,
And
Mental illness is not just being SAD